# PRAISE FOR ANNE WHITEHOUSE'S POETRY

## THE REFRAIN

"It is a pleasure to read poetry so independent of reference; her symbols, often drawn from nature, are developed integrally, in the way for example of Baudelaire, with his indelible image/symbol of a swan struggling in the dust, who happens to be one of the few poets to whom Whitehouse refers….In *The Refrain,* form and content have met." **-Ron Gaskill**, *Jerseyworks*

"Whitehouse writes of aging; death; art; music; writing; dreams; nature; animals; birds; gardening; seasons; relationships between wife and husband, mother and daughter, bride and groom, friends; and more. And she relates these topics to changes and choices she - or one - has in life, love, relationships, etc. With articulate description and imagery, Whitehouse's poems have unique insights." **-Pam Rosenblatt**, *Boston Area Small Press and Poetry Scene*

"Anne Whitehouse portrays herself in each word. As if the words were simply meant to be in the order she places them — they beg, they ask her to piece together a puzzle, which soon transforms into a masterpiece. We see this masterpiece as we reflect upon the cruel and truthful words from "Meditations in June" — Anne exposes life, even from the view of others:

*The world is a terrible place.*
*There's no getting out alive,*
*Said my friend from his hospital bed.*

As this truth pours out onto the table, as these words meet the eyes, I find that Anne is exactly what she is. No matter how you take these words from *The Refrain*, she is what she is; whatever you portray her to be.

*I-am-what-I-am.*" **-Josh Hess**, *Decades Review*

"Wallace Stevens says in 'Anecdote of the Jar,' 'It made the slovenly wilderness/ Surround that hill/…no longer wild.' He adds that the jar was 'a port in air,' as are Anne's poems ports in air, windows bringing in and letting out, but ports as safe harbors, sanctuaries, that hold and organize parts of a terrifying and chaotic world."   -**Jeffrey DeLotto**, *Gently Read Literature*

"A house struck by lightning, a bed-bug infestation, the onset of dementia, a bird trapped in a house, a child trapped inside her parents' squabbles—all of these moments effect a mysterious change, a new and clearer vision. Like novelists Virginia Woolf and Laurie Colwin, Whitehouse scans quotidian detail for her metaphors, and like them, she always selects the resonant image that, without commentary, gives meaning to the whole. As a poet, however, Whitehouse can tell a story and develop a character in just a few charged lines. As with a great novelist, empathy is the keynote of Anne Whitehouse's vision as her poems take the reader into momentous crossings in the lives of others.… Reading *The Refrain* is a rewarding and humanizing experience, like the experience of reading a good novel. We enter the lives of others in language that allows us to connect with and appreciate their challenges, broadening and deepening our own humanity."
   -**Mary Kaiser**, *Alabama Writers Forum*

"Anne's themes are eternal ones: the inevitable passage of time in a human lifetime and the power and fragility of human memory. From page 1's 'Choices Apprehend You' with its meditation on Saint Sebastian—'Eternity's magic lived in his future'—to the last page, where appears the book's title poem and its 'life and death' and 'life-in-death' juxtaposition, we join the poet's contemplation of mortality, confronting our own and our loved ones' with Anne as our guide and comforter."
   -**Karla Linn Merrifield**, *The Centrifugal Eye*

## ONE SUNDAY MORNING

"Within the pages of this spellbinding collection, there's an undeniable perplexity and wonderment when observing realities beyond our power....The central theme woven throughout the book is that nature, with its beauty, banality and grandeur, can also be chaotic, unpredictable, and cruel....Granted, this message may be age-old, but the ingenuity in Whitehouse's delivery defies stereotypes, making it fresh and new....There does not seem to be one extraneous poem in the collection."
     -**Cheryl Sommese**, *The Write Place at the Write Time*

"The poems shatter all expectations, as Whitehouse explores everything from death to love to nightmares. Continuously drawing us in with their sharp images of place and time, the poems bring to life the sensations of the speaker and offer surprising glimpses of the seemingly familiar through an innovative eye.... Balancing her personal, reflective speaker with her precise, luminous images, Whitehouse delivers a chapbook that is much more than a simple "Sunday morning" read.... Whitehouse startles as much as she satisfies and adds a strong volume to her growing body of work."     -**Jill Neziri**, *Editions Bibliotekos*

## BEAR IN MIND

"Anne Whitehouse's 'The Beyond,'—and we say this with confidence—stands alone, and is perhaps one of the best 9/11 poems that we have read. It is truly an exceptional poem—the control exercised by the poetic voice on such a subject of apocalyptic chaos, yet the tenderness and the emotion—with depth as deep...as T.S. Eliot or W.B. Yeats....Through her poetic voice we understand the human (the poet's) predicament and predilection—the act of searching, for something new, to reclaim what has been left behind for us to find."
                    -**Gregory Tague**, *Editions Bibliotekos*

## BLESSINGS AND CURSES

"Whitehouse crafts quietly elegant poems in which the seemingly simple surfaces contain striking profundities and deeply felt experience. These poems literally glow from within. And nowhere is she more eloquent than when describing the intensely isolating challenge of rendering words, work that is at once unforgiving and divine, that can engender as much nostalgia for what has been lost as pride for what has been accomplished. How fortunate for readers of contemporary poetry that Whitehouse has assembled such an accomplished and engaging meditation on life's meanings and its accompanying troubles. 'Her abiding wish / was to instruct by delight,' the poet writes of a pianist she once knew. The same can be said for this profound and delight-full collection."
-**John Vanderslice**, *Santa Fe Writers Project*

"Anne Whitehouse's gentle understanding alternates with her astringent anatomizing of character—the mix produces a deeply humane volume that's a bold change from the weightless irony and knowingness of postmodernism."
-**David Castronovo**,
author of *Blokes: The Bad Boys of British Literature* & other books

## PRAISE FOR ANNE WHITEHOUSE'S NOVEL, *FALL LOVE*

"Whitehouse's poetic handling of language and of sensuous detail is superb: in her descriptions, especially, of the intimacies of lovemaking, she is at the same time graphic and subtle, provocative and sensitive; in her portrayal of the unspoken emotions - about death and its aftermath, of fear, of pride, and of hurt - she conveys powerfully the cruel effects of all those coincidences of life." -**Elaine Hughes**, *First Draft*

"The main characters in Anne Whitehouse's novel, *Fall Love,* are Althea, Jeanne, Paul, and Bryce: four twentysomethings in New York in 1980. And while we meet other characters over the months that the novel takes place, as I read, I found myself feeling that one persistent theme was so integral that, to me, it almost functioned as a character as well. The idea of what it means to be an artist is a theme impels the action throughout the novel and that is returned to again and again in different ways...The initial questions of identity are still there at the novel's end, and if progress has been made, it is uncertain progress. And I didn't really feel as if the story ended: only the part of it that I had been watching."  **-Jennifer Finstrom**, *NEAT*

# METEOR SHOWER

poems by

## Anne Whitehouse

DOS MADRES

2016

## DOS MADRES PRESS INC.
P.O.Box 294, Loveland, Ohio 45140
www.dosmadres.com    editor@dosmadres.com

Dos Madres is dedicated to the belief that the small press is essential to the vitality of contemporary literature as a carrier of the new voice, as well as the older, sometimes forgotten voices of the past. And in an ever more virtual world, to the creation of fine books pleasing to the eye and hand.

Dos Madres is named in honor of Vera Murphy and Libbie Hughes, the "Dos Madres" whose contributions have made this press possible.

Dos Madres Press, Inc. is an Ohio Not For Profit Corporation and a 501 (c) (3) qualified public charity. Contributions are tax deductible.

Executive Editor: Robert J. Murphy

Illustration & Book Design: Elizabeth H. Murphy
www.illusionstudios.net

Typset in Adobe Garamond Pro, Saginaw & Gill Sans Light
ISBN 978-1-939929-60-0
Library of Congress Control Number:  2016947598

*First Edition*

# ACKNOWLEDGMENTS & NOTES

Grateful acknowledgment is made to the following journals and anthologies where these poems first appeared:

*A Narrow Fellow: Journal of Poetry, Agave Magazine, Alabama Literary Review, Avanim, Boston Literary Magazine, The Basil O'Flaherty, Bray Arts Journal, The Buenos Aires Reader, By&By Poetry, Chagrin River Review, Connotation Press, Contrary Magazine, Cyclamens and Swords, Decades Review, Driftwood Press, The Fieldstone Review, The Front Porch Review, Ginosko Literary Journal, Granny Smith Magazine, The Greensilk Journal, Halcyon, Hamilton Stone Review, Handsy, Healthy Artists, Indian Review, IthacaLit, Jerseyworks, The Left Hand of the Father, The Linnet's Wings, Lyric, Magnapoets, Manhattanville Review, Mason's Road, The Metric, NEAT Mag, Niche Literary Magazine, Northern Cardinal Review, Oddball Magazine, Poetic Medicine, Poetry Pacific, Poplorish, Rasputin, Resurrection Review, Review Americana, Riverbabble, Saranac Review, Scythe, Sick Lit Magazine, Songs of Eretz Poetry Review, The Literary Nest, The Stillwater Review, The Thing Itself, Transient Publishing, Vermont Literary Review, Vine Leaves Literary Journal, Works& Days Quarterly, The Write Place at the Write Time, The Write Room, Young Ravens Literary Review, Your Daily Poem, Zingara Poet.*

Translation from Bernart de Ventadorn by W.S. Merwin. Reprinted with permission from *The Mays of Ventadorn*. Copyright © 2002 National Geographic Society.

A note about the events that inspired "The Eye that Cries:" "Organizers and militants of *Sendero Luminoso*, or the Shining Path, Peru's notorious guerrilla movement, waged armed conflict from the early 1980s until the mid- 1990s. By then, the government had captured and jailed much of *Sendero's* top leadership. The conflict claimed almost 70,000 lives and destroyed and displaced entire communities. Both *Senderistas* and the army conducted massacres.....The vast majority of those who lived in terror and with terror were indigenous peasants of the Peruvian highlands, physically and socially quite distanced from the dominant Peruvian metropolis of Lima....'The memorial [i]s a beautiful, arresting sculpture that powerfully evoke[s] the suffering of all Peruvians who continue to struggle through painful reconciliation in the wake of the terrorism and violence.'" -Katherine Hite, *"The Eye that Cries:" The Politics of Representing Victims in Contemporary Peru. A Contra Corriente.* Vol. 5, No. 1, Fall 2007, 108-134 http://www.ncsu.edu/acontracorriente/fall_07/Hite.pdf

"My Cuba" was suggested by "Sweet and Savory Memories Caramelized in Exile," by Alex Witchel, of Ana Sofía Peláez, author of The Cuban Table: A Celebration of Food, Flavors, and History. *The New York Times*, 10/31/14, p.C30.)

"After the Apocalypse", Chuck Berry. "Go go go Johnny go." *Chuck Berry is on Top.* Chess Records, 1959. Album.

For my publishers, Robert and Elizabeth Murphy

and for Stephen and Claire, again


*Chantars no pot gaire valer,*
*Si d'ins dal cor no mou lo chans!*
*Ni chans no pot dal cor mover,*
*Si no i es fin' amors corau.*


*No use singing, it seems to me,*
*unless the song comes from the heart,*
*and song cannot come from the heart*
*unless true love is there already.*

-Bernart de Ventadorn,
translated by W.S. Merwin

# TABLE OF CONTENTS

## I

## A Girl Who Fell in Love with an Island

1   A GIRL WHO FELL IN LOVE WITH AN ISLAND

3   ON VACATION

4   SCENES FROM CALIFORNIA

6   AT THE OCEAN

7   STORY OF A DRESS

8   IN OLD ENGLAND

10  FIRES OF YOUTH

12  AN AFTERNOON NAP

13  ONE SUMMER DAY ON THE NUMBER ONE TRAIN

15  ONE-WAY SESSION

## II

## The Eye that Cries

19  THE EYE THAT CRIES

21  MOTHERS OF SUICIDES

22  LOL

23  MY LAST SPRING IN MY HOUSE AND GARDEN

24  MY CUBA

25  A FEW THINGS I LEARNED FROM MY MOTHER-IN-LAW

27  READINGS

29  POET IN NEW YORK

30  ELEGY (FOR WENDY)

31  INSPIRATION

# III
# Moving

35  MOVING

36  CONTRARIES

37  WEDDING SILVER

38  A SISTERLY CONFESSION

39  A BACKWARD GLANCE

40  THE "E-E-E-E-E"

42  MY FATHER'S PHOTOGRAPHS

44  ONE STEP AHEAD

45  REGRET

46  DELETE, DELETE

# IV
# The Mask

49   THE MASK

50   ZEN RIDER

51   LESS IMPACT

52   WAITING

53   CREATIVITY

54   TWO VARIATIONS

55   TWIN DANCERS

56   AFTER THE PERFORMANCE

57   SMOKE AND FOG

# V
# Grout Pond

61   GROUT POND

62   THE SECRET

63   NOURISHMENT

64   HIGH SUMMER

65   SHADOWS

66  LUMINESCENCE

67  AUTUMN LIGHT

68  WINTER SILENCE

69  DUST MOTES

# VI
# Life's Continuous Chain

73  LIFE'S CONTINUOUS CHAIN

75  GLIMPSE OF GLORY

76  FINITUDES

78  CALLIGRAPHIES

81  BOOKENDS

84  AFTER THE APOCALYPSE

85  METEOR SHOWER

89  About the Author

# I

# A Girl
# Who Fell in Love
# with an Island

# A GIRL WHO FELL IN LOVE
## WITH AN ISLAND

I thought I saw the ghost of myself
as I was at the age of 27,
standing up on a bicycle, peddling uphill,
long hair streaming behind her.
She smiled as she passed me in the twilight
and wished me a good evening.

On the back of her bike was
a milk crate for hauling things,
the same as I once had.
She was wearing flip-flops
and a loose wrapped skirt.
I had seen her on the beach,
making salutations to the setting sun
over the sea in a reflected fire
of blazing gold and rose embers.
I hadn't wanted to interrupt her,
or show her to herself thirty years older.

I was a girl who fell in love with an island.
Each time I've left here,
something of that quiet, introspective girl
has lingered behind and never left.
On visits when I come across her
she has never gotten any older.

In August I return in search of her,
wearing my oldest clothes, ones she wore,
worn and faded, softened by use.
Once again she and I are one
when I swim in the cove's cold waters,
gazing up at the sea and sky
or diving underwater to watch
the dark kelps waving over the rocks.

# ON VACATION

The lifted white tail
of a deer glimpsed at dawn,
whoosh of raised hooves
and uneven thuds
as it vanishes into the brush.

A ribbon of fog
lies over the marsh
like a vestige of a dream,
dissolving so rapidly
in the wakeful sun
it seems it never existed.

Like an empty vessel
the day waits to be filled
as we did half our lives ago
biking up and down hills
bumping over stones
skidding over sand
and not falling
swimming in the sea
and resting in the sand
our bodies alive to each other
and to every living thing.

# SCENES FROM CALIFORNIA

## I Elk In Fog

To think that diaphanous fog
could obscure
so massive a creature
silhouetted against the horizon
as if far away,
while the ocean, veiled in mists,
roared against the cliffs.

## II Trapped Cow

Somehow it slipped
down the muddy gulley
and couldn't climb out.
A man out hiking
heard the bellowing
and summoned the farmer
who shot the animal
out of mercy.
Surprisingly preserved,
its body leans
against the incline
like a black shadow,
its unseen feet resting
in shallow water.

## III  Life/Land Forms

The slopes of the headlands
slide smoothly to the sea
of cold waters and roiling tides.

Under a wet shock of brown grass,
the narrow skeleton of a fox,
where weeds blow back yellow and russet,
and coots align in even rows
across the rippling surface of a pond.

Past mossy trees tangled in vines
and lichen-covered fences of an old farm,
lies a ribbon of brown sand
without beginning or end.

# AT THE OCEAN

A soft breeze blows
through my baggy clothes,
awakening my skin like a lover.
Every leaf and blade of grass
is in motion,
every nodding wildflower
beckons me to the cove,
where the sea washes over the rocks,
and the wet sand is printed
with the tracks of waterbirds.

The tide is coming in,
and I am almost too late to swim out
to the rock I have always swum to—
carpeted with soft seaweeds,
purple and green, that I hold onto
like Rapunzel's hair, and climb
until I stand up free in the air
as the day I was born.

Soon the rock will be buried
in the dark sea.
But I find my balance,
grip the seaweeds with my toes,
while the cold water washes
over my ankles and splashes my shins.

# STORY OF A DRESS

I remember that sleeveless summer dress
with wide stripes of mauve,
magenta and blue Marcia gave me,
loose and comfortable
with deep pockets and no zipper.
I slipped it over my head,
pulled my arms through the armholes,
and that was it.

But one day my daughter said,
"Lose it, Mom. I hate that dress on you."
So I packed it with me to Cartagena
and in the Hotel de Tres Banderas,
wore it to breakfast one morning.
Lidia, who worked there, admired it.
I returned to my room, reappearing
in pants and a tee-shirt
and gave her the dress on a hanger,
happy at the thought
of it swaying gently over her hips
as she crosses a sun-dappled plaza
shaded by palms.

# IN OLD ENGLAND

The sun was at its most restful level,
just before sunset when its rays are slanting,
and everything glows. The yellow stone
of the parish church seemed warm and alive,
and the gravestones in its ancient yard
threw long shadows over the mounds.

I never saw such a patched-up church,
a mixture of styles, each one
interrupted by an addition
before it had a chance
to follow out its lines.
Arches grew out of each other
like suckers on a stump;
its windows had grown cataracts
and were quite blind.

I walked to the village in the evening,
and from a distance the sight
of the spire felt momentous,
the yew trees black
against an electric blue sky
where one star twinkled
past the tip of the steeple.
I thought, if only I could play piano
the way I felt, I'd be worth listening to!

It felt romantic to walk up and down streets
where the half-timbered houses
were blue in the twilight,
and here and there a light shone in a kitchen
where a table was laid for supper.

That night I lay in bed in a brown room
and watched the moon come up
over my windowsill,
and the next morning the sun
did the same stunt in the same place.

# FIRES OF YOUTH

First we are children, experiencing life
unfolding from within,
events superseding one another,
blotting out much of what went before,
save for those eternal moments
that remain in the adult mind years later,
suspended like insects in amber,
fixed outside the flow of time.

When we have our own children,
we are given a chance to live childhood over
achingly aware of how transient it is—
mysterious life with its pangs and pleasures
coming from us, flowing out of us.

And when the raising of our children is over,
and they set out on their own lives,
we are aware of life passed as if in a dream—
our mortality, our lost vitality.

Then how much more beautiful
to see from the aspect of age
the fires of youth brightly glowing
in the five teenaged violinists
in glittering gowns the colors of roses,
their dark, silken hair pulled back in ponytails,
playing out their hearts like virtuosos—

Debussy, like the siren's piercing song,
winding its tentacles through the hearts
of the old people in the audience,
who then listened intently, with fading senses,
to Mozart's crystalline joys,
and Bach's bracing sonorities
breaking into Amazing Grace.

# AN AFTERNOON NAP

I lay slipping into sleep
as a delicious breeze washed over me,
blown in from the sea, warmed by the land,
clear and sparkling, yet soft as a caress.

From the open window, I thought
I heard a voice calling me
"Mama!" through the green summer,
across the long years.

Sunwashed, seastruck, windswept,
Sunstruck, seaswept, windwashed,
Sunswept, seawashed, windstruck.

In contentment I lay, not wanting to rouse,
in delicious reverie, as if drunk from lovemaking,
languorous and mellow, ready for the fall.

# ONE SUMMER DAY
## ON THE NUMBER ONE TRAIN

When the doors of the express opened at 72 Street,
the local was waiting. She entered with me,
tall and angular as a crane, her expression alert,
violin poised against her clavicle like a wing.

The train was half-empty, the passengers dozing
or absorbed in their smartphones.
She stood at one end of the car, her gaze
swiftly appraising us, while the doors slid shut.

Closing her eyes, she lifted her bow
and dipped her chin, and into that pause
went all the years of preparation
that had brought her to this moment.

The train accelerated in a rush of cacophony,
her music welled up, and I recognized
a Bach concerto blossoming to fullness
like an ever-opening rose. Suddenly

I was crying for no reason and every reason,
in front of strangers. I thought of the courtroom
where, an hour ago, I'd sat listening to testimony
with fellow jurors, charged to determine the facts

and follow the law. But no matter how we tried,
we couldn't reverse damage or undo wrong.
The music was contrast and balm, like sunlight
in subterranean air. The tears wet on my cheeks,

I broke into applause, joined by fellow passengers.
We'd become an audience, *her* audience,
just before the doors opened and we scattered.
Making my offering, I exited, too shy to catch her eye.

But she'd seen the effect her music had wrought.
Its echo resounded in my memory, following me
into the glory of the summer afternoon.
It is with me still.

# ONE-WAY SESSION

*in memory of Marc Snyder*

By the time we heard
your phone message
canceling our meeting,
you had died.

You were our therapist
for 25 years—
to think I still believed
we had all the time
in the world!

All the time
to resist and avoid
our most painful truths.

Only you had the ability
to turn our gazes inward
to reveal how we'd each
wronged the other.

You knew the worst about us
and liked us in spite of it.
I imagine speaking to you,
trying to hear your answer:

*"He's not asking
you to fix his problem,
but just to listen,
try and understand."*

15

From deep within
I feel the release from
that old way of being,

as if at last I swam out
from under the rock
that had trapped me,

and let myself be pulled
by a silken current
to those places
where we find each other
and hold on,

swaying with each other,
our grip loosening
and tightening and loosening
and tightening

like the way we love to float
in the sea, on our backs,
our legs entwined,
me inside my love,

the two of us warm
and steady, for this time,
now and forever,
between the two immensities.

# II

# The Eye That Cries

# THE EYE THAT CRIES

*Memorial to the victims of Peru's internal armed conflict*
*1980-2000 by Lika Mutal, Dutch-born Peruvian sculptor,*
*installed in Campo de Marte, Lima, Peru*


After such conflict,
there is only this quiet space,
not a bridge, but a separation, like a moat,
between what cannot be, and what is.

Past a grassy knoll, in the heart
of the labyrinth's circuit,
sits the ancient, jagged stone of Mother Earth
in a pool formed by the spill of water
forever flowing from her rocky eye.

The twisting journey of reflection
leads each soul in single file
along the path of collective memory
bordered by thousands of identical stones.

Here every eye-shaped stone
is inscribed with a name and date,
even if names and dates are a way
not to remember, but to forget
what part in the fight each one took.

Those strangers with dark, wrinkled faces
and bowler hats, their legs bowed
as if they'd just stepped off a ship
into the fogs of the coastal capital,
and not traveled down from distant highlands
where the air is thin and cold and hard to breathe,
and legacies of violence live on side by side.

It wasn't so much what they'd come to find
as what they'd come to lose—
that instinctive fear, like an animal's,
giving off a harsh scent.
Knowing that their grief
at last can speak its name.

# MOTHERS OF SUICIDES

The mothers of the suicides
wear downcast looks years later.
The skin of their faces sag,
the corners of their mouths are etched
in expressions of permanent discontent,
hollows of sadness form around their eyes.

Their sons took their lives at home,
in early manhood. One hung himself
in the garage; his sister found him.
The other waited till the family left
for a reunion he'd refused to attend,
arranged himself in an armchair,
and slit his wrists. It was a hot week,
and the smell from the apartment
alerted the neighbors.

Worse than the dread were the discoveries.
The nightmares have never gone away.

*What do you want from me?*
*You were the one who left—*
*Why won't you let me go?*
*Whatever I did that was wrong,*
*I'm still paying for it.*

# LOL

She signs her texts and emails
Laughing Out Loud
but inside she is crying,
slowly dissolving herself
into a thinner and thinner shell
riddled with hairline cracks.

I worry she will desiccate, disintegrate.
I pray that day doesn't come.
Every time I read
a text of hers with that phrase,
I am consumed by dread.

# MY LAST SPRING
## IN MY HOUSE AND GARDEN

I planted my sanctuary
for a future I will not see—
where I lived for 35 years,
where I'd hoped to grow old.

I sit motionless under the trees
and watch my blossoms falling
and bruising on the ground.

If I could, I would slip
into the soil like a buried seed.
Instead I am being blown far,
far away—I, who always
clung so close to home.

When he walked out of the marriage,
it was as if lightning struck our oak,
splitting it in half, not cleanly,
but with spikes and jagged edges.

No more soaring trunk,
no more roots in this fertile earth,
watered by my tears,
sparkling in the spring sun.

# MY CUBA

My grandparents left Cuba in the early sixties;
they never imagined the revolution would last.

After the Cuban missile crisis, they realized
they were cast out of Eden. Decades passed.

At last I went for a visit and found a time warp.
People living in the past, without technology

or the usual stream of new possessions.
Instead, the patched and mended predominated,

nostalgic and dilapidated in the brilliant sun.
Alone, at a café in Havana, surrounded by tourists,

I fought back tears as I listened to a song
my grandparents sang, and it seemed

as if someone I knew might walk in the door.
But no one came. An impossible thought,

like the idea of the life I might have had,
had my grandparents not left. Yet I have grown

at peace with the Cuba they gave me.
I carry their homeland lost and found in my heart.

# A FEW THINGS I LEARNED
# FROM MY MOTHER-IN-LAW

*In memory of Martha Jane Linton Whitehouse*

Every day for a little while, it's fun to sit and do nothing.
The more you know about the natural world,
the more delight it gives you.
To hide a feeling is not dishonest,
it can be a way to protect and honor it.

I had not grown up in a family that respected boundaries,
and it was a relief to have a mother-in-law
who set such store by them.
In her I found a kindred spirit
who understood the pleasures of solitude,
altering her mind with the flow of the world.

Life is here one day and gone the next.
Enjoy what life offers you, but don't make too much of it.
If you live in a nice house, you can have a nice life.
Eating and drinking are two of the great joys of life.
Smoking is another, but you can do without it.

History is an anchor, and family history is a key.
Try not to be needy, but have compassion for those who are.
Value education, and honor those who provide it.
Do your work quietly, don't make a fuss.

If you love a complicated man, you will learn to adapt.
You can afford to let him be more serious than you are.
There is nothing more important than family,
even if your family sometimes drives you crazy.

Martha, mother-in-law, gin-drinker, I lift
my glass to you, bare-footed, braving the humidity
on the porch, armed with your frosty martini,
watching the surface of the canal stained pink
by a pastel sunset through dark palms,
blurred by the passage of underwater life.

Your voice quavers slightly as you relate
a tale of your husband's mother's father—
an orphaned twelve-year-old farmed out to relatives
who beat him, he ran away and apprenticed himself
to a blacksmith and, by the end of the summer,
he'd learned to lift the heavy sledgehammer standing on his toes.

So that long-vanished ancestors will come to enlighten us,
you tell us the family stories you have taken to heart.

# READINGS

### I

Sometimes I'll be reading
and come to a description
or a way of looking
I'd thought was mine alone
written by someone I've never met,
perhaps someone long dead,
and the connection forms a bridge
out of myself to guide me back.

### II

What Shakespeare was to Larry,
the grasslands were to his father,
a great, subtle text rewarding endless study.
His father had a countryman's eye
for small varieties of landscape.

Larry looked at many places quickly.
His father looked at one place deeply.
Each year the short drive on the dirt road
to the ranch became less of a simple thing.

III

After nightfall
I watch a yellow half moon
suspended above the horizon
before it slips behind the sea
fading light in the starry black sky.

When we look at the heavens,
we see into the past
through time light takes to reach us.

# POET IN NEW YORK

*In memoriam, Federico García Lorca*

The long June evenings hide secrets--
new life shadowed by green leaves,
messy and wet, delicate and fragile.

On my way to a concert in the falling dusk,
I pass doormen standing one by one
in the entrances along Seventy-Eighth Street
singing love songs in Spanish and Italian.
Like awnings that shelter the singers,
the rain makes spaces for their melodies.

I am thinking of Lorca on his birthday,
spiritual descendent of gypsies and troubadours,
and how he came to New York
fleeing the wreckage of love
and friends who called his art old-fashioned.
The city was the remedy he let explode
within him in all its mysterious force,
its hurts were wounds to lead him to creation.

# ELEGY (FOR WENDY)

*In memory of Wendy Caplin*


Your expressive brown eyes
with their faint tinge of hurt,

on a blue-and-white island in the Aegean,
on a beach honeycombed with caves,

one summer in your reckless youth—
no clothes but a caftan, a rock for your roof.

Lulled by breezes, rocked by waves,
you danced in the sea, water sparkled on your skin.

In the film that your friend made of you,
you seemed more alive than I will ever be.

There are other films—yours, too—
all the films are now your ghosts.

Of films that took shape from your editing touch,
I am drawn to the Tibetan throat singers,

how they trained their vocal cavities to produce unearthly tones,
like the growl of a bull united with the song of a child.

Watching, listening, I am shaken to the core
by the tantric voice vibrating in rhythm with the universe.

# INSPIRATION

I was death-haunted
and tried not to know it.
I walked along the park's promenade,
my landmarks hidden in white mist
and melting snow, like a dream
where figures appeared out of nowhere
and passed in silence.

Once Rilke replied
to a tedious business letter,
lay his head down on the table,
and heard the voice resonating in his mind,
*Who, if I cried out, would hear me among the angels' hierarchies?*
*Every angel is terrifying*, he heard,
imagining that annihilating embrace
empowering the *Duino Elegies*.

Sailing against the wind,
when you capture the resistance,
you can sail faster than the wind itself.

In seconds the fog lifted—
one moment visible
and vanished the next
from a rise in temperature.

Inspiration is everywhere and nowhere,
as diffuse as moonlight,
present as the hum of a refrigerator,
or the silence when the refrigerator
shuts off.

# III

# Moving

# MOVING

First memories are moving targets—
what the four-year old recalls,
the ten-year-old may have forgotten.

The processes of recollection
are constantly forming
deep within the brain
inside the bony ridge named for a seahorse.

Tracks lie on top of other tracks,
twisting and turning on themselves,
until we lose the reasons
why we became what we are.

# CONTRARIES

Fifty years ago my sister
got stung by a jellyfish,
and she hasn't gone back in the ocean.
I've never been stung so much
that I wouldn't go back.

In green waters suspended with sand,
soft-bodied swimmers I cannot see
brush against me as I glide by.

Just imagine—not ever going under,
always in air and not in water,
never feeling the wonder
of an alien element all around.

# WEDDING SILVER

Reed and Barton, Pointed Antique—
our wedding silver, plain and timeless.

My mother's pattern—
that's why I selected it—

because she promised her silver to me,
to fill out my collection.

Only after she died I learned
that she'd sold it instead.

At some point she'd changed her mind
and carried out her plan in secret—

leaving this bitter surprise
as her legacy.

# A SISTERLY CONFESSION

Starved for all
you have excluded
from your life,
you confide how
loneliness and misery
overcomes you in closed rooms.

In funereal black for our father,
your skin stretched tight
across your forehead,
like an immigrant ancestor
accustomed to deprivation—

You tell me that nothing I tell you
can make your life better.
You don't want advice,
but what is rarer—sympathy.

Sometimes, with others,
I notice that something pent-up
from under great pressure
rushes out of you,

and your voice is like a waterfall
trying to drown out
the threatening world
in the cocoon of your own sound.

# A BACKWARD GLANCE

In tiny color transparencies,
these images swim up from the past
into the oval of my magnifying glass:

My grandparents squint
into the sweltering Alabama sun
next to long-lost relatives
visiting from Australia.
I am eight years old.

My mother lounges by the pool
in a one-piece bathing suit
looking younger than I remember
on a Florida vacation,
while my sisters splash in the pool.
I am thirteen.

Flash forward half a dozen years
to my sisters holding bouquets
as if they were bridesmaids
standing next to their dates at a dance
under an arch twined with artificial flowers.

In these captured moments
everyone is always smiling,
and yet I want to weep
for what will happen to us,
for what has happened already.

# THE "E-E-E-E-E-E"

The sound could be long and drawn out
like a hissing wind—
e-e-e-e-e-e-e-e—
or short and staccato
like eruptions from the gut—
eee-eee-eee-eee-eee.
I don't know how it started
among us four siblings
but I know how it grew.
It sounded like so many things—
fear, enthusiasm, excitement—
but what it really meant was danger.

We thought it kept us safe
but in the end
it prevented us from saying
what we wanted to tell each other.
I think we were afraid
we would speak truths
that we could not unsay
about our parents and ourselves,
and love would vanish like evaporation.
And so one of us would go,
e-e-e-e-e, and another
would pick it up and carry it
like a round to the next.

The themes and variations
kept us going for years.
It meant everything,
and it meant nothing—
our secret childhood language
unleashed of words—
an unbearable sorrow
without explanation.

# MY FATHER'S PHOTOGRAPHS

My father took beautiful pictures
of my sisters and me when we were children—
with his Hasselblad, his Rolleiflex,
his Leica, his Minolta, his Kodak.

He developed film and made prints
in his makeshift darkroom in the basement
next to the laundry sink and washing machine,
below the pegboard hung with tools.

There he installed a long table with a trough
of galvanized steel that drained into the waste line.
With a hose he ran water from the sink,
and there he put trays of chemicals—
developer, stop bath, fixer.

He set up the enlarger, hung the safelight,
covered the slits of light under the doors
with black oilcloth, and in the cool darkness
he spent hours away from us, absorbed in us.

I have his eight-by-ten-inch prints
scanned into my computer—
In one, I see a dreamy, pensive girl,
sitting up straight on a stool,
hands folded in her lap, hair combed
back and held with a barrette.

In another, I stand next to my sister
with my doll in my arms, smiling
in front of the carport's cinderblock wall.
In my favorite, my next sister,
a toddler, welcomes the last sister,
a newborn just home from the hospital.

My father's pictures record his devotion
to us. Later, when things went wrong,
his photography became intrusive,
hostile, no longer a gesture of love.

Instead of posing us with care in natural light
and rendering us in subtle black-and-white,
he lurked on the sidelines of family gatherings,
hiding behind his lenses, which he thrust
in front of our faces, startling us
aggressively with the blinding flash.

Those are the pictures I will not scan—
where we appear paralyzed and stunned
like animals trapped in front of headlights
on a dark country road at night.

# ONE STEP AHEAD

All my life I've stayed
one step ahead
so as not to fall behind
and be overtaken
by the living nightmares
that pursue me.
If they caught me,
they would drag
me down, down,
down to a dark place
where I couldn't escape.

So I keep ahead of myself,
out of sync.
Always planning the next phase
before the current one's complete,
trying to dodge the traps ahead
while fleeing the terrors behind.

# REGRET

"Anne goes about all day with her head in the clouds."
How these words of my mother's mother hurt me
when I read them twelve years after her death
in a letter she'd written to her brother, dead now too.

I'm shocked by her tone of querulous complaint.
I'd never known she disapproved of me.
Accused, I feel maligned, misunderstood.
Yet wonder, was she wrong, or was she right?

It's like the sting of a dead bee I once stepped on
in the surf, that I never thought could harm me,
but my toe swelled up red as fire, in astonishing pain,
and I couldn't walk on it for several days.

In vain I rehearse replies in self-defense,
as if I could respond to her long dead and gone:
"Look how I've taken care of myself and others, too;
Look how I've lived within my means, and I've survived."

But I've had to change myself to be this way.
I feel the hollow ache of a queer regret
for what I've had to lose as I've grown older,
and that I couldn't tell her, that she couldn't see.

## DELETE, DELETE

I log on to email every day.
My inbox is full of offers, appeals,
advice, updates, reminders—
I go through the list, reading
and deleting, or deleting
without reading.

My brain has reached capacity
and is starting to shrink.
I try to delete more than I add
to the heavy baggage of self.

Delete the urge to suffer
that twisted me in knots,
delete the need to be right,
to have the last word,
to have my own way.
Knowing I cannot choose
the way my life will end.

# IV

# The Mask

# THE MASK

The walrus ivory is stained dark
from long burial in the earth.
It will never be white again.

The animal face catalyzes
spirits deep within us.

Shadows come alive,
and a night-veiled girl
dances in a circle of light.
Like smoke above a fire,
she sways and dissolves.

Wisdom is in the knot
threaded through the mask,
the braided tassel trembling
on its own, without a touch
of hand or air.

# ZEN RIDER

Caspar is a great jumper
but all who try to ride him
end up in his favorite ditch.
At last it is my turn.

From the quietest place in my heart
I tap into his will and his need,
at one with the pulse of his breath
as he gallops across the fields.

## LESS IMPACT

I want to live gently,
step lightly,
treading softly
for those
who come after,
leaving more
of the earth
less trampled.

Relaxing my grip
on the things
of the world,
I feel myself
softening
into the earth,
dissolving
into the air.

# WAITING

Much of life is waiting—
for the train, for the plane,
for the light to change.
Moving and waiting.

Stirring the pot
while the food cooks.
Waiting for the bell
to end the class,
for the workday
to be over.

As a math student
I used to fall asleep
on a problem I couldn't solve,
willing myself to dream the answer,
and sometimes I did.

# CREATIVITY

Your mistakes will force you
beyond imagination
to something new.

You will deny your teachers,
betray your influences, turn away
from the past that constrains you.

An accident will lead you to creation.

# TWO VARIATIONS

## I   Leaves In A Wind

Dried husks of
once living selves,
they blow up
and whirl
following the will
of the wind
in spirals
cold and dark
to ice and snow
until at last
they fall
to rest.

## II   A Fire In Winter

Perhaps there is a blaze left in me yet
as I move toward my evening.
I want to dance like a flame,
light and graceful as leaves in a wind,

blown up and whirling gaily,
up and down, easy as you please,
as careless as a girl with youth to spend,
till I fall at last and come to rest.

# TWIN DANCERS

After the twins fed the alpacas
and walked them around the pen,
brother and sister would sit in silence
perched on the fence, watchful
in the New Mexican desert,
the only children for miles around.

A decade later, transformed
into tall and graceful dancers—
a stillness lingers about them.
Within their movements, a space opens,
revealing a further space beyond.

# AFTER THE PERFORMANCE

*for Lauren Flanigan*

The stage was a vast seashell
where music like water left
a taste of salt, a fairyland
alive with malicious laughter,
and she its source—
limpid beauty with a demon's tongue,
a mermaid who swam in from the sea.

Silver hair freed, soaked
and plastered to her head,
her shining face scrubbed of make-up,
in black sweats she goes out
to walk her dog that patiently
waited all this time.

# SMOKE AND FOG

On one side of the road
was ice and fog,
on the other, smoke and fire.

We were driving by the river
while the fire burned above us
a quarter-mile away.

Cool on the driver's side,
and on the passenger's,
the closed window glass
was hot to the touch.

Suffocating smoke
billowed into the air,
suffusing the atmosphere
like waterless blood.

The river was clogged
with floes of ice
melting in a sudden thaw.

Drawn out of the snowmelt,
a hazy fog hung low
over the water.

Above our heads,
above the roof of the car,
the smoke from the fire
met the fog off the ice.

The road took us
straight up the middle,
as if that were a choice
we were free to make.

# V

# Grout Pond

# GROUT POND

In a bowl between mountains
the pond mirrored the sky:
reflections of clouds
and the blue dome of space

on the wrinkled fabric
of the water's surface,
where the wind raised whitecaps,
and the sun sparkled like sequins.

Down a road nearly 200 years old
meandering through a forest,
I saw a moose munching apples
in an abandoned orchard.

Witness to secret silences,
a pilgrim to forgotten places,
I listened carefully to what
was not heard elsewhere.

# THE SECRET

A cleft in the hillside
opens to a sandy beach
that reveals others' secrets—
discarded clothing,
a child's toy half-sunk in sand—
and beyond, the spreading lake,
still as glass.

The wind in the trees says nothing
over and over again.
On the ground
lie fallen apples
tipped gold in rising light.

# NOURISHMENT

*Pt. Reyes, California*


Sweetwater oysters grilled in their juices,
hot sauce and sourdough bread,
and raw oysters trembling in the shell,
piquant with lemon, consumed in a swallow.

Mushrooms simmered in a brown sauce,
wild rice and salad greens, olives, oranges,
and wine—those virtuous transplants—
and tender cheeses, shaped lovingly by hand.

# HIGH SUMMER

A dragonfly darts around a water lily

Whine of insects
Meadow grass, thigh-high

So hot the pine boards sweat
In the airless loft of the barn

What relief to sink into
Cold Cobb Brook---

My hair fanning around me.

# SHADOWS

The stone garden lingers like a shadow
reflected in the depths of her eyes.

The shadows of water spiders
lie on the sandy stream bed
like black petals.

Here, in the heart of the forest,
cleft by a waterfall,
the sun's heat never penetrates.

# LUMINESCENCE

pink perigee moon of August
scent of wild rose and honeysuckle

where fireflies dance in the grass
and frogs croak in the swamp

swallows are flying to roost
barn owls are flying to hunt

bluefish and stripers run in the floodtide
churning the surface of the sea

comb jellies bob in the currents
their tiny combs refracting moonlight

underwater rainbows
shimmering in liquid darkness

# AUTUMN LIGHT

A faint breeze ruffles
the last leaves on the trees,
and a parade of dead leaves
skids over the dry dock,
light enough to float
over the surface of the quarry
with its deep, dark waters.
The sky has opened up,
beautiful and terrible.
It is time to go.

# WINTER SILENCE

Black wasp creeping
across the floor
too weak to fly.

Spider thread
so fine it can't be seen
except in slanted light

crossing the artist's easel
unused for the past century
since his death.

Scattered illuminations
from fragmented lives.

# DUST MOTES

Early January, snowed under.
The sky deep blue as a flower
where the Nosterkill rushes under ice
in the direction of all streams
that join greater waters.

Inside, I was washing my hair
at my weekend routine,
blissfully soaking in a warm bath,
as I rinsed off soap and shampoo.

Where light fell in slanting shafts
to lie in squares on the green floor,
I saw colonies of dust motes,
twirling, falling, rising.

So many they were myriad,
yet I never knew
they were always there
trapped in light and air,
unfelt, unheard, unseen.

# VI

# Life's
# Continuous Chain

# LIFE'S CONTINUOUS CHAIN

The music of wind in trees
and rain across wet grass
binds me to earth and its abundance—
every vine, leaf and flower vibrant
along this path where I have gone in trouble
for the wind to ease my sorrow,
or in despair until it seems
the red sunset is my own blood
dissolving into the night.

The swamp is a reflecting pool
stained dark by leaf droppings,
where light falls in silvery shafts,
and the shadows are emerald green,
like longings from childhood
that begin and end in mystery.

Below dark, glossy leaves,
under a tangle of vines,
a dappled pattern catches my eye—
a wild sow lies nested
at the base of a magnolia,
breathing deeply, absorbed in rest.
At a little distance is her litter,
a mass of shifting bodies,
birth-damp still upon them.
One piglet, pied black,
with a white band around its middle,
wriggles out from under the others

and wobbles to the sow's side.
It gives a delighted whimper,
and the rest of the litter
ambles over to discover
the miracle of the hairy breasts.

A silent pulsing, steady and vital,
by dark, shining waters,
under rustling leaves.

# GLIMPSE OF GLORY

*in memory of Hellen Zeanah Macon Cherner*

The day before my grandmother died,
the glare of reflected sunlight
on the window of her hospital room
was so bright that I had to look away.

She gazed at the clock on the wall,
at my two-year-old playing beside her
on the bed, and her face lit up.

When she spoke she was a nurse again,
contented in her place of work,
her soft voice dispensing lovingkindness.

I'd been thinking she was getting better.
I know now it was the opposite—
her spirit was readying for the infinite.

# FINITUDES

### I

Leaves fall like confetti. In gusts,
they twist and turn. The hawksbill geranium
we planted in July is still blooming in October,
each tendril ending in a violet flower.
Low to the ground, nodding softly
in the wind, it never seems to struggle.

### II

Under a weightless rain,
in dress uniforms of dark blue,
the firemen marched in solemn step
to the mournful accompaniment
of the "Emerald Society Pipes and Drums."
Wreaths were laid at the monument,
and a bell struck for every man lost
in the last year.

Our dead are always with us,
not only at anniversaries.
They keep watch over us,
they chide and encourage us,
if we let them.

## III

It was a day like any other day,
the mist hung low to the ground
and hid the hills.
The wind blew and the rain spilled,
and the sun broke through.
And the wet grass waved,
as majestic clouds floated past,
like time, hurrying
in one direction.

## IV

The migrating bird that can't keep up
gets left behind.

Bathe me in golden light,
heal my shattered bones.

# CALLIGRAPHIES

*for Cai Guo-Qiang*

In the old days in China
my father collected calligraphy,
ancient scrolls, and rare books.
We lived in Quanzhou,
across the strait from Taiwan.
We could hear artillery batteries
firing into the mist at the island
that still resisted the mainland.

My father's calligraphy
was delicate and adept.
I used to stand at his shoulder,
careful to leave space
for his arm to move freely,
as I watched him wet the ink
to the right consistency,
select his brush, and dip it
gently and carefully, soaking
the soft hairs of the badger,
and stroke its sides
against the jar, forming a point
like no other, soft, flexible, yielding.

With an intake of breath,
he raised his hand that held the brush,
hovering above the paper,
and slowly exhaled
until he was an empty receptacle,

and then, and only then,
he touched the tip of the brush
to the fine rice paper—
the strokes flowed, deft and sensitive,
forming the ancient shapes of the words.

Then came the Cultural Revolution.
My father worried that his books,
his scrolls, and his calligraphy
were a time bomb ticking.
He buried his collection in a hole
in the earth of the cellar,
but he was still afraid, and little by little,
he began to burn it, at night, in secret,
in the hidden depths of the house.

Afterwards he was not the same.
He lost himself in a strange self-exile
and left us all, his family, behind,
finding perilous refuge
far away in the mountains
in a ruined Buddhist convent,
where an old crone of ninety,
the last remaining resident,
gave him sanctuary.

There he would take sticks
and write calligraphy once more
in puddles on the ground
that would disappear
as soon as it was written,

leaving invisible skeins of sorrow
in the changing reflections
of cloud and sky on water.

I am his son, and my calligraphy
is fireworks, my art gunpowder,
as evanescent as writing on water.
*Pinyin*—the Chinese word
means fire medicine, invented
by alchemists investigating immortality.

My explosions are brief dreams,
where space and time combine
in a momentary universe
of birds, fish, and animals,
little-known symbols,
the stream of the Milky Way,
energy transformed into chaos.

In my youth a shaman protected me
from the ghosts of dissatisfaction
that were haunting me,
freeing me to communicate
the invisible within the visible.
Some mysteries are meant to be discovered,
some are meant to remain heaven's secrets.
I imagine an alternate history
where the discovery of nuclear power
was not used for making weapons.
I dream of creating a ladder of fire
far in the air above the earth,
seen from worlds beyond our own.

# BOOKENDS

*In memory of my father-in-law, Hugh Lord Whitehouse*

### I

For days we'd been packing—
the clothes that would fit no one
had been given away,
the rooms were full of boxes
and tagged furniture,
the walls were bare,
closets and cupboards empty.

Yet, stripped of so much,
the house still enchanted us,
enfolded and protected us.
Light through dozens of windows
played over the clean white walls
and stairs and banisters of maple wood.
At the back of the house was the view
over the watery road of the canal
and all the wildlife that lived along it.

The night before the movers came
I made a dinner of triple tail
baked with butter and lemon,
roast potatoes and asparagus,
green salad with tomato,
avocado, and goat cheese—
one last meal to add to
the memorable meals over the years.

Later that night I swam in the pool
in the warm September rain,
while my husband shot pool
in the next room.
Through the glass doors I glimpsed him
aiming the cue, heard
the clicks of balls being struck.
I dove underwater,
submerged in a sweet,
prolonged farewell.

Dense night, falling rain
on warm water, the air so full
of rain it was like water.

II

Just before everyone left,
I discovered the bookends
interspersed between the books
that no one was taking

and recognized my father-in-law's handiwork
in the blocks of wood four inches square,
each fastened at right angles with two screws
to a square of aluminum.

Made with care, using materials at hand,
the squares of wood sanded and stained,
and the squares of aluminum sanded, too,
so they would slide smoothly
between book and bookshelf.

Presented with the bookends,
my husband dated them from his father's
grad student days, when short on money,
with mechanical abilities and cultivated tastes,
he made a pair of floor lamps
from salad bowls and ski poles painted black,
with tubular linen shades.

In so much of what he did,
My father-in-law exhibited a painful perfection
that was hard to live up to, hard to live with.
In their serenity and simplicity,
these beautiful objects he made
reveal nothing of his struggles.

# AFTER THE APOCALYPSE

Back then they thought
that if the human race was doomed,
at least they'd be preserving
an archive of earthly sounds
on a gold-plated record
aboard the Voyager spacecraft,
like a message in a bottle
tossed into outer space
for extraterrestrials to discover
on the far shores of the universe
on a happier planet than ours,
these last traces of our lives:
beatings of a heart,
soft *mwah* of a mother's kiss,
sounds of wind, crashing surf
and falling rain,
footsteps and laughter,
the cry of a chimpanzee,
Bach's harmonies
and Mozart's melodies
and Chuck Berry singing
"Johnny B. Goode:"
*Go go go Johnny go—*
unfaded echoes
of our lost existence.

# METEOR SHOWER

We lie on blankets in the grass
grateful for the scratchy wool
in the sudden chill of night
deep within the virgin forest
at a family reunion far from our homes.

Scanning the sky for falling stars—
there goes one! and there another!
Persistent trains, bright fireballs—
in the great immensity
a crescent moon crosses to Jupiter,

and snatches of conversation fly up
more intimate now
we are hidden in darkness
and can express what
we might not say otherwise.

At every instant we are
what we have been and will be,
our forebears who live on in us
we remember, we resemble.

Everything in the world is mysterious
formed of tenuous substances
evanescence and oblivion
the equivocal element of time.

With a stone I dug up a clod of dirt
a little farther away I laid it down silently
and under my breath I whispered
"*I have changed the earth.*"

The deed was minimal, the words exact,
and I needed a lifetime to say them.

# ABOUT THE AUTHOR

ANNE WHITEHOUSE was born in Birmingham, Alabama,  and grew up there during the civil rights era. She graduated from Harvard College, where she studied with Octavio Paz, Robert Fitzgerald, Robert Lowell, and Jane Shore. She went on to receive an MFA in creative writing from Columbia University. Her thesis, advised by Charles Wright, became her first collection of poems, *The Surveyor's Hand*. More than 25 years passed before her second collection. But the muse had not entirely deserted her; *Blessings and Curses* was published by Poetic Matrix Press in 2009, followed by Finishing Line Press chapbooks, *Bear in Mind* and *One Sunday Morning*, in the next two successive years. In 2012, Dos Madres Press published her full-length collection, *The Refrain*, a culmination of poems going back three decades. Now, four years later, Dos Madres is publishing her new collection, *Meteor Shower*.

Anne Whitehouse's novel *Fall Love,* originally published in 2001, is enjoying a second life as an ebook. It is available as *Amigos y amantes* in Manuela Canela's Spanish translation published by Mundi Books Ediciones. Her poems and short stories have appeared in literary magazines throughout the English-speaking world from England to India. Her book reviews and feature articles have been published in major newspapers throughout the U.S. She is a winner of the 2015 Nazim Hikmet poetry competition and the 2016 Common Good Books' poems of gratitude contest. Her poem, "On the Osa," received the 2016 RhymeOn! poetry award, and her poem, "Calligraphies," was awarded the 2016 *Songs of Eretz* poetry prize. She lives in New York City.

# BOOKS BY DOS MADRES PRESS

## ❯2004
Annie Finch - *Home Birth*
Norman Finkelstein - *An Assembly*
Richard Hague - *Burst, Poems Quickly*
Robert Murphy - *Not For You Alone*
Tyrone Williams - *Futures, Elections*

## ❯2005
Gerry Grubbs - *Still Life*
James Hogan - *Rue St. Jacques*
Peter O'Leary - *A Mystical Theology of the Limbic Fissure*
David Schloss - *Behind the Eyes*
Henry Weinfield - *The Tears of the Muses*

## ❯2006
Paul Bray - *Things Past and Things to Come*
Michael Heller - *A Look at the Door with the Hinges Off*
Michael Heller - *Earth and Cave*
Richard Luftig - *Off The Map*
J. Morris - *The Musician, Approaching Sleep*

## ❯2007
Joseph Donahue - *The Copper Scroll*
Pauletta Hansel - *First Person*
Burt Kimmelman - *There Are Words*
Robert Murphy - *Life in the Ordovician*
William Schickel - *What A Woman*

## ❯2008
Michael Autrey - *From The Genre Of Silence*
Paul Bray - *Terrible Woods*
Eric Hoffman - *Life At Braintree*
Henry Weinfield - *Without Mythologies*

## ◗ 2009

Jon Curley - *New Shadows*

Deborah Diemont - *Wanderer*

Norman Finkelstein - *Scribe*

Nathan Swartzendruber - *Opaque Projectionist*

## ◗ 2010

Gerry Grubbs - *Girls in Bright Dresses Dancing*

Michael Henson - *The Tao of Longing & The Body Geographic*

Keith Holyoak - *My Minotaur*

Madeline Tiger - *The Atheist's Prayer*

Donald Wellman - *A North Atlantic Wall*

## ◗ 2011

Pauletta Hansel - *What I Did There*

Eric Hoffman - *The American Eye*

David M. Katz - *Claims of Home*

Burt Kimmelman - *The Way We Live*

Bea Opengart - *In The Land*

David A. Petreman - *Candlelight in Quintero-bilingual ed.*

Paul Pines - *Reflections in a Smoking Mirror*

Murray Shugars - *Songs My Mother Never Taught Me*

Madeline Tiger - *From the Viewing Stand*

James Tolan - *Red Walls*

Martin Willetts Jr. - *Secrets No One Must Talk About*

Tyrone Williams - *Adventures of Pi*

## ◗ 2012

Jennifer Arin - *Ways We Hold*

Jon Curley - *Angles of Incidents*

Sara Dailey - *Earlier Lives*

Richard Darabaner - *Plaint*

Deborah Diemont - *Diverting Angels*

Richard Hague - *During The Recent Extinctions*

R. Nemo Hill - *When Men Bow Down*
W. Nick Hill - *And We'd Understand Crows Laughing*
Keith Holyoak - *Foreigner*
Pamela L. Laskin - *Plagiarist*
Austin MacRae - *The Organ Builder*
Rick Mullin - *Soutine*
Pam O'Brien - *The Answer To Each Is The Same*
Lianne Spidel & Anne Loveland - *Pairings*
Henry Weinfield - *A Wandering Aramaean*
Donald Wellman - T*he Cranberry Island Series*
Anne Whitehouse - *The Refrain*


◖◗2013

Mary Margaret Alvarado - *Hey Folly*
John Anson - *Jose-Maria de Heredia's Les Trophées*
Gerry Grubbs - *The Hive-a book we read for its honey*
Ruth D. Handel - *Tugboat Warrior*
Eric Hoffman - *By the Hours*
Nancy Kassell - *Text(isles)*
Sherry Kearns - *Deep Kiss*
Owen Lewis - *Sometimes Full of Daylight*
Mario Markus - *Chemical Poems-One For Each Element*
Rick Mullin - *Coelacanth*
Robert Murphy - *From Behind The Blind*
Paul Pines - *New Orleans Variations & Paris Ouroboros*
Murray Shugars - *Snakebit Kudzu*
Jason Shulman - *What does reward bring you but to bind you
    to Heaven like a slave?*
Olivia Stiffler - *Otherwise, we are safe*
Carole Stone - *Hurt, the Shadow-the Josephine Hopper poems*
Brian Volck - *Flesh Becomes Word*
Kip Zegers - *The Poet of Schools*

## ▶2014

John Anson - *Time Pieces - poems & translations*
Ann Cefola - *Face Painting in the Dark*
Grace Curtis - *The Shape of a Box*
Dennis Daly - *Nightwalking with Nathaniel-poems of Salem*
Karen George - *Swim Your Way Back*
Ralph La Charity - *Farewellia a la Aralee*
Patricia Monaghan - *Mary-A Life in Verse*
Rick Mullin - *Sonnets on the Voyage of the Beagle*
Fred Muratori - *A Civilization*
Paul Pines - *Fishing on the Pole Star*
Don Schofield - *In Lands Imagination Favors*
Daniel Shapiro - *The Red Handkerchief and other poems*
Maxine Silverman - *Palimpsest*
Lianne Spidel & Anne Loveland - *A Bird in the Hand*
Sarah White - *The Unknowing Muse*

## ▶2015

Stuart Bartow - *Einstein's Lawn*
Kevin Cutrer - *Lord's Own Anointed*
Richard Hague - *Where Drunk Men Go*
Ruth D. Handel - *No Border is Perennial*
Pauletta Hansel - *Tangle*
Eric Hoffman - *Forms of Life*
Roald Hoffmann - *Something That Belongs To You*
Keith Holyoak - *The Gospel According to Judas*
David M. Katz - *Stanzas on Oz*
Sherry Kearns - *The Magnificence of Ruin*
Marjorie Deiter Keyishian - *Ashes and All*
Jill Kelly Koren - *The Work of the Body*
Owen Lewis - *Best Man*
Rick Mullin - *Stignatz & the User of Vicenza*
Paul Pines - *Message from the Memoirist*

Samantha Reiser - *Tomas Simon and Other Poems*

Quanita Roberson - *Soul Growing-Wisdom for thirteen year old boys
from men around the world*

David Schloss - *Reports from Babylon and Beyond*

Eileen R. Tabios - *INVENT[ST]ORY Selected Catalog Poems and New 1996-2015*

Kip Zegers - *The Pond in Room 318*

◖2016

Eduardo Chirinos - *Still Life with Flies [naturaleza muerta con moscas],*
Bilingual, English translation by G. J. Racz

Norman Finkelstein - *The Ratio of Reason to Magic: New & Selected Poems*

Gerry Grubbs - *The Palace of Flowers*

R. Nemo Hill - *In No Man's Ear*

W. Nick Hill - *Blue Nocturne*

Sharon Olinka - *Old Ballerina Club*

Natalie Safir - *Eyewitness*

Daniel Shapiro - *Woman at the Cusp of Twilight*

Anne Whitehouse - *Meteor Shower*

Geoffrey Woolf - *Learn to Love Explosives*

David Almaleck Wolinsky - *The Crane is Flying - Early Poems*

www.dosmadres.com